MW01628851

Hey,
Corona!
Who Are You
Anyway?

ISBN 978-1-68025-130-2

Contact Chaim Walder at:
Office: 972-3-5618722 / Cell: 972-50-4133075 / Fax: 972-3-6779944
office.walder@gmail.com

To send stories for Kids Speak and People Speak:
Chaim Walder, POB 211, Bnei Brak, Israel
or: wold10@bezeqint.net

Distributed by:
FELDHEIM PUBLISHERS
POB 43163, Jerusalem, Israel

208 Airport Executive Park
Nanuet, New York 10943

Distributed in Europe by:
LEHMANNS
+44-0-191-430-0333
info@lehmanns.co.uk
www.lehmanns.co.uk

Distributed in Australia by:
GOLDS WORLD OF JUDAICA
+613 95278775
info@golds.com.au
www.golds.com.au

Printed in USA

Illustrated by Yaakov Chanan
Book design by Y. Shneidman
Project manager: Moshe Walder
Translated by Aviva Rappaport
Proofread by Cindy Scarr

Chaim Walder

Ahuva Raanan

Hey, Corona!

Who Are You Anyway?

FOR KIDS & PARENTS

DISTRIBUTED BY
FELDHEIM

Dedicated with love

to children everywhere
and especially to the children of
Bnei Brak** & **Telz-Stone
(because that's where we live…)

CHAPTER 1

What Is Corona?

Corona is a virus
that you can't even see.

Only doctors and other professionals, using a special tool called an “electron microscope,” can see it.

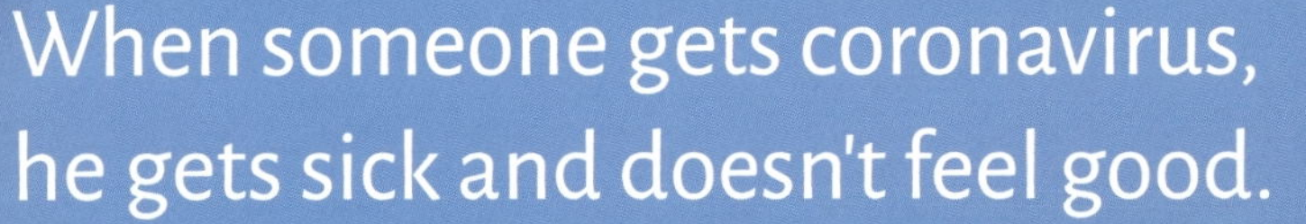
When someone gets coronavirus,
he gets sick and doesn't feel good.

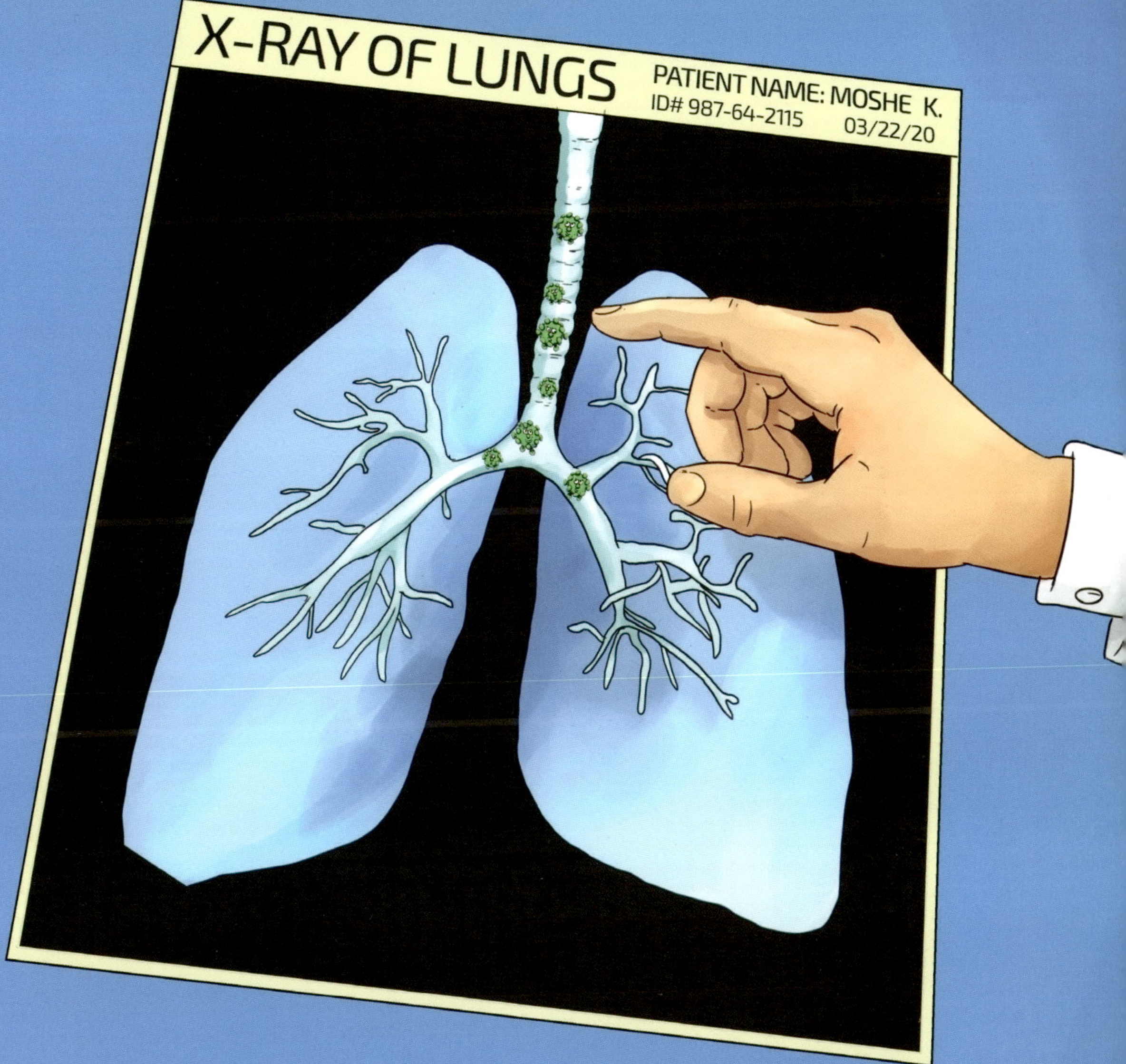

He might get a fever and have a cough
and have trouble breathing
(because the virus affects the respiratory system).

Most people who get sick with the coronavirus are sick for only a short time. They feel only a little bit sick until, *be'ezras Hashem*, they recover and are healthy again.

CHAPTER 2

Why Is Everyone So Afraid of the Coronavirus?

There are two main problems with the coronavirus.

The first problem is
that it's very contagious.

When a person has coronavirus
and he gets close to a person
who doesn't have it—
especially if he touches him
or breathes near him—
then the coronavirus passes to
the other person.

The second problem is that
some people who catch it—
very few, and mostly older people—
can have serious breathing problems
(that can even, *chas v'chalilah*, cause death).

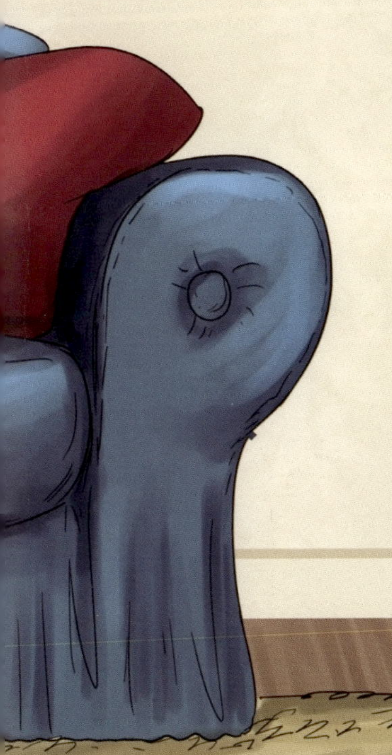

CHAPTER 3

How Can We Win the War against the Coronavirus?

To keep the coronavirus
from spreading really fast,
and making lots of people sick,
we all have to help.

We need to make sure
it doesn't infect lots and lots of people,
so doctors can take care of the people
who are seriously ill.

So what should we do?

We should stay at home and not go out.

That's why we're not going to school or the playground or friends.

(The *Gedolim* even said that people should learn Torah and pray alone.)

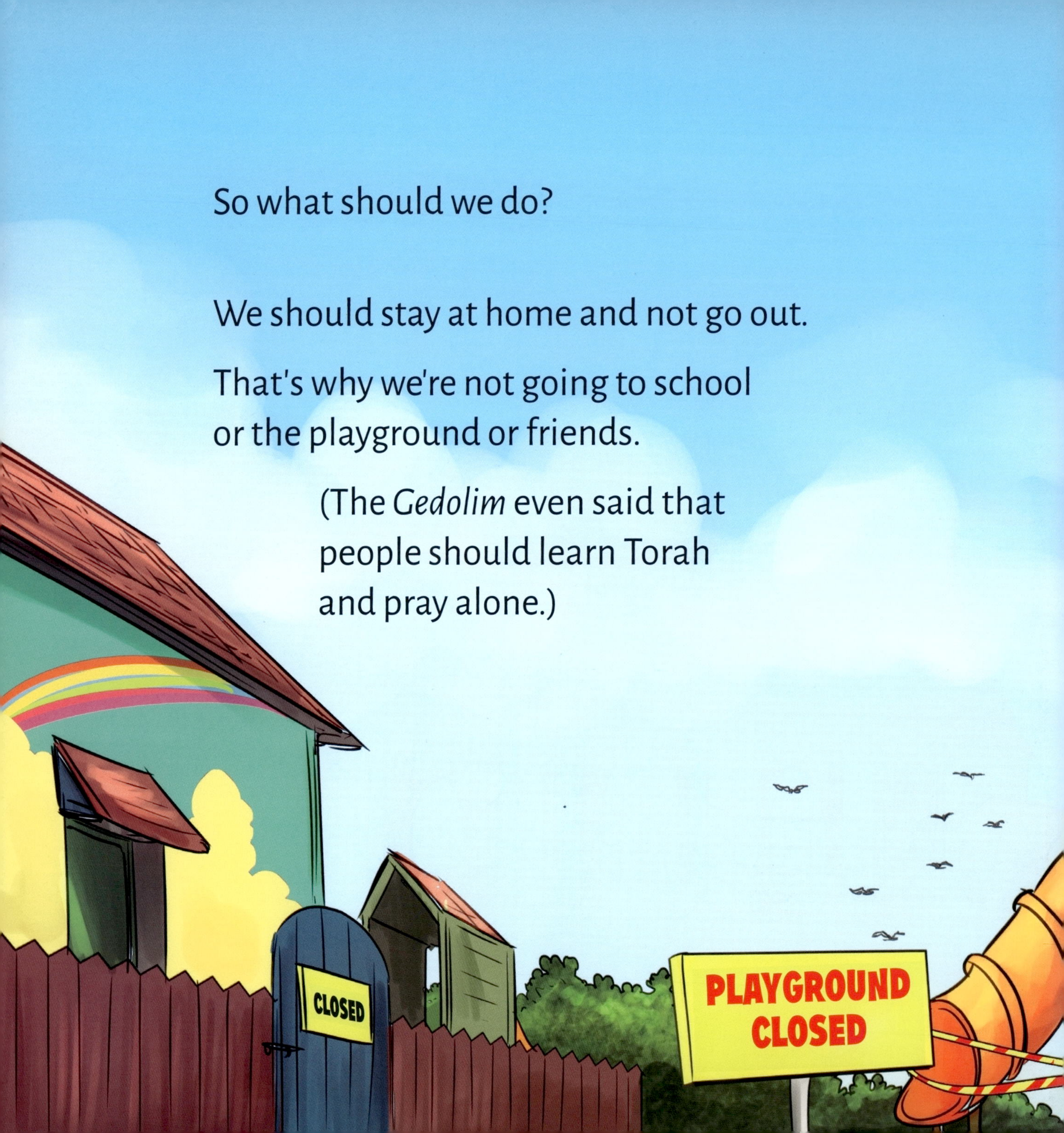

CLOSED

Because of this, the health department
ordered anyone who was near
someone who got sick
with the coronavirus
to stay home for two weeks,
without going outside.

(It's called "self-isolation.")

We also need to maintain cleanliness
by washing our hands with soap
for 20 seconds,
especially before we eat
and after we use the bathroom.

And if we need to sneeze or cough,
we should first
cover our nose or mouth
with a tissue.

Whoever does this
gets a big mitzvah:

Venishmartem me'od lenafshosechem
(taking very good care of your health).

If you see people
wearing a face mask
or disposable gloves,

it's because they are trying to make sure
they don't catch the virus
(adults call this “hygiene”).

CHAPTER 4

Until We Defeat the Coronavirus, What Can We Do?

Until the spread of the coronavirus stops,
(soon, *be'ezras Hashem*),
and fewer people are catching it,
    no one is going to school,
    and there's lots of free time at home.

So what can we do?

A good idea is to plan with your parents
what to do every day.

We can divide the day into three parts
and do some important things
and some fun things in each part.

(This is called "making a schedule.")

Vacation Schedule

Morning:

- Wake up (*netilas yadayim*, brush teeth, get dressed)
- Daven
- Breakfast
- Clean room
- Workbook or coloring book
- Exercise
- Snack (fruit)
- Building toys (Legos)

Afternoon:

- Lunch
- *Tehillim*
- Draw
- Read or listen to music
- Play a game
- Snack (vegetable)
- Word or number games
- Helping around the house
- Free time

Evening:

- Supper
- Shower
- Brush teeth
- Talk with parents
- Story
- Shema
- Good night

Work on staying in a good mood and being friendly.

It's really important
to stay calm and happy,
to honor your parents, and
to be nice to your siblings.

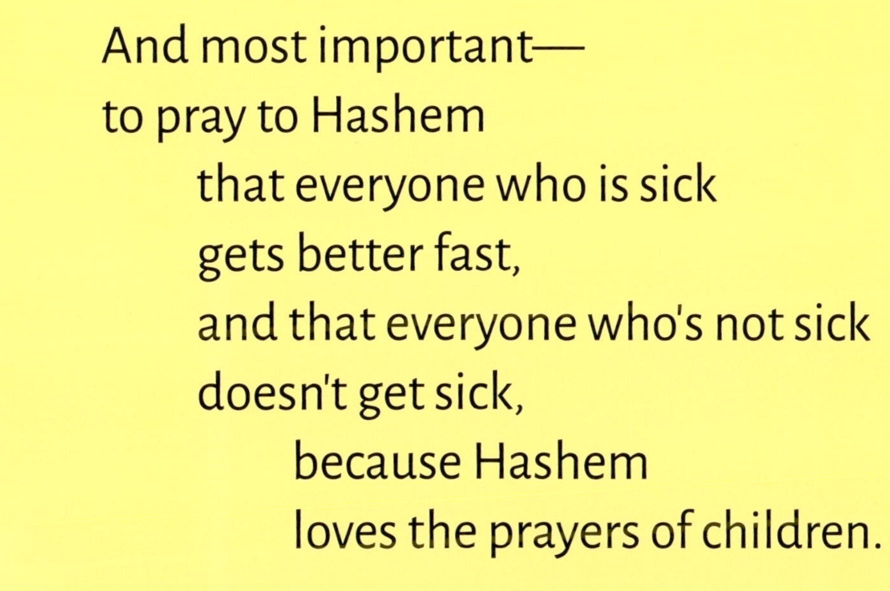

And most important—
to pray to Hashem
that everyone who is sick
gets better fast,
and that everyone who's not sick
doesn't get sick,
because Hashem
loves the prayers of children.

Parenting in the Shadow of Corona

ESSENTIAL KNOWLEDGE AND ADVICE FOR PARENTS

Being a Parent
During the Corona Crisis

In times of uncertainty and stress, parents play a major role.

Parents are the ones who mold their child's reality. They shape in their child's brain his understanding of current events. They even have it within their power to pave the way for their child to cope with the accompanying challenges.

Many things are not under our control in this turbulent time. Still, we can work to help our children to navigate the period safely and to cope with all its various aspects in an effective and healthy manner.

Unfortunately, much of what is happening outside our homes is not in our control. We can't control the rate at which the virus spreads, the government decisions on whether schools are open, our income at this time, and much more.

But we can certainly shape matters at home to express our values during this period. These include the daily routine, the atmosphere, family members' moods, the information children see and hear, and the degree of closeness and support we give each other.

What Is Our Role as Parents?

INFORMATION BROKERS

- **Give Age-Appropriate Information**

  Give your children clear, reliable, and accurate information but without unnecessary details. The information should explain the various concepts children have heard about in today's confusing reality, and explain the reasons for the guidelines and restrictions imposed on us to keep us healthy.

- **Control the Flow of Information**

  It is best not to expose children to information they don't need to know, or that's inappropriate for their level of emotional development. If and when they encounter stressful or painful information, it is essential to explain it to them in a calm, truthful manner.

- **Distinguish between Rumor and Fact**

  It's good to ask a child what they know or think about the coronavirus. Doing so allows us to understand what their concerns are, to distinguish rumor from fact, and to give them the information they need to know.

TRUST, CLOSENESS, AND SECURITY

- **Open Communication**

  It's a good idea to have a brief daily talk with your children about their feelings. Doing so allows for the recognition of emotions such as fear, trepidation, anxiety, stress, boredom, and confusion. Talking openly like this gives children the feeling they're understood and supported and that there is a listening ear to which they can talk about their fears and worries.

- **Convey Confidence in Your Child's Ability to Cope**

  Children need to feel that we are confident both in our ability as a family and in their abilities as children to cope with the challenging situation.

  Optimistic and reassuring remarks convey a message of hope, of a temporary crisis that will pass, and of encouragement—as opposed to warnings, threats, and intimidation, which discourage.

  Likewise, a focus on following the safety regulations is calming and encouraging.

  ("What can we do to stay healthy? We obey the health department's instructions on staying home, washing our hands well, covering our nose and mouth when we cough or sneeze, and disinfecting surfaces. We pray for a speedy recovery for all the people who are ill...." Remarks like these convey the optimistic message that we are handling the situation well.)

- ### Maintain Routine and Assign Chores

  Routine gives children security and a sense of control, which is why it's essential to maintain the regular family routine as much as possible.

  It's a good idea to keep children on a regular age-appropriate schedule that includes schoolwork, physical activities, helping around the house, and play and other fun activities. The satisfaction that comes from completing simple assigned chores or offering to help gives a child a feeling of security and control and enhances their sense of belonging to the family.

- ### Keep in Touch When Apart

  Encourage your child to call his grandparents and friends and to listen to the teacher's phone messages. Doing so will help them feel close to people who are distant due to the current situation.

Even if **your child is in quarantine**, make sure to put these principles into action. They will help him deal with the isolation more easily.

These measures will, with *siyatta diShemaya*, keep our children calm, give them a sense of security and belonging, and let them know they can trust us to help them navigate this complex period.

With prayers for good health,
and with warm wishes for calm and peaceful days!